The Power of Change

Understanding Your Resilience in the Midst of Growth

Dr. Angel Barber Jackson

Honey Tree Publishing, LLC
Louisville, Kentucky 40215
www.honeytreepublishingus.com

Copyright © 2019 by Dr. Angel Barber Jackson
ISBN: 978-0-9910318-7-0
First Edition- 2019 (paperback)

All rights reserved. No part of this book may be used or reproduced in any manner whatsoever without written permission, except in the case of brief quotations embodied in critical articles and reviews. For information address Honey Tree Publishing, LLC. All scriptures are from the New Living Translation.

Library of Congress Cataloging-in-Publication Data
Jackson, Dr. Angel Barber, 1985

The Power of change: Understanding your resilience in the midst of growth

By. Dr. Angel Jackson

Cover Photo: Dr. Angel Barber Jackson
Cover and Interior by: Tytianna N.M. Wells
Printed in the United States of America

Acknowledgements

"For I know the plans I have for you," declares the LORD, "plans to prosper you and not to harm you, plans to give you hope and a future." Jeremiah 29:11 (NIV)

First and foremost, I would like to give an honor to the man above. I most certainly would not be who I am and would have not been able to experience this journey without Him.

Second, I would like to thank my husband Brandon for taking the time to listen and shower me with love and encouragement without judgement. To my two beautiful and strong children Emerald and Braxton. Thank you for allowing me to be your mother and blessing me in more ways than you two could ever imagine.

To my Barber family - I would like to thank my parents George and Stephanie for loving me and teaching me to always trust in the Lord. The life lessons that you all taught me, have helped me to grow in various ways and I thank you. You all are truly the best parents in the world. To my brother George and sister Cortney, thank you all for always believing in me and telling me I can do it!

Last, but certainly not least, I would like to thank my grandparents Rev. Larry and Vivian Lewis for showing me what love is. To my late grandmother Granny Carolyn I love you. To my aunts, uncles, and cousins, you know I have nothing but love.

Family, recognize that you are Kings and Queens and to never settle. Always follow your dreams and trust the process. Know that God is with you and He will never leave you nor forsake you.

This book is dedicated to the one who inspired me the most, my uncle Travis "Looney" Jackson. Thank you for reminding me that in the world of education, I can and will make a difference too. You are never forgotten and will always be in my heart.

A poem to my friends:

To those who have experience heartache and pain.
To those who never broke their silence and is still holding on to life's pain.
There is healing in your experiences and healing in your journey.
Trust the path and know that you are resilient.

    With Kindness,

    Angel

Table of Contents

Introduction- The Five C's……………..………....1

Chapter 1- Compassion…………….....................3

Chapter 2- Communication………………………19

Chapter 3- Collaboration……………………....30

Chapter 4- Commitment……………………......35

Chapter 5- Consistency……………………….41

Conclusion……………………………………….52

Introduction

There are 5 C's that lead to a systematic change: **Compassion, Communication, Collaboration, Commitment, and Consistency**. These 5 C's must be acknowledged in order for a positive change to happen. This change can pertain to relationships, marriages, weight loss, healthy eating, promoting a positive mindset, and goal setting. For this to occur, you must have the outlook of growth. During a period of growth, you will experience change on many levels!

This period of growth also means that you are experiencing some healthy wins. All wins regardless if they are small or large, are just that— a win! You wake up to see another day, it is a win! You— landing your dream job, it is a win! You— exercising for thirty minutes, it is a win! No matter how you arrive at your destination and/or milestone, it is a win. Believe me we all want to experience a win! This win means that you are one-step closer to completing the goal that you set out to achieve. This, my friend, is perseverance.

In life, you are going to go through some tough times. You are going to have some trials and tribulations. I like to call them tests. When you are being tested, you must continue to push regardless of how you may feel or what people may say. During these times, you learn to trust the process and begin to change your perspective from negative to positive. This is when you begin to understand your resilience because you are elevating to your highest level of spiritual and mental growth.

Throughout my life, I have learned that with resilience comes with one being willing to give up a little of ourselves to know more of ourselves. Now, I know this may be a hard concept for some to realize, but we as humans must take hold of the light that we have within ourselves and be willing to share that light with others without judgement.

That is my hope for this book, as it is a little glimpse of how I overcame trauma at a young age, and now, as an adult, I am healing. When society labeled as me as another statistic. But, God! This book will provide an outlook of the importance of setting the stage for an authentic and transparent approach to creating change in relationships with our loved ones.

As you read this book, my prayer is for you to press forward to discover your fullest potential. Let the seeds of these words bring you understanding and enlightenment to a woman's journey. A woman who understands the concept of resilience in the midst of trials and tests. Trust and believe that nothing happens by accident. One can learn and grow in all experiences. Realize that your journey is your journey. Embrace it and own it. My friend, trust the process and trust the journey.

Chapter 1

Compassion

"Be kind, for everyone you meet is fighting a harder battle." - Plato

Momma said there will be days like this. Shoot and my momma wasn't lying. My momma would tell me that there would be times in life that I would be tested, but I would have to persevere. Growing up in a two-parent home was definitely a blessing. I learned so much from my parents, with compassion being one of the main attributes. My mom and dad always told me that they loved me. They showed me through the sacrifices they made to make sure that I had what I needed. The skills that my parents taught me throughout my younger years have helped me to grow and mature into the woman that I am today. They taught me the importance of loving myself, being kind to others, trying my best, and to never give up! While my parents taught me many lessons, the most important one was to have a strong foundation in Christ. I learned that whenever I was tested, it was important that I went to my foundation and to seek the word of God like never before.

I had a yearning thirst to receive healing and peace for my life. I never thought that in my early thirties, I would receive healing from the trauma and insecurities that I dealt with as a young girl.

First, I had to discover compassion for myself. I then realized that compassion was a doorway to change, which allowed me to have a profound perspective about my life.

When I look back, I am reminded of how God continued to show compassion towards me. It was His grace and mercy that saved me.

God continued to wrap His loving arms around me and comfort me. He provided me with strength when I was weak. When I messed up, he continued to forgive me and reminded me that I am His. When I am reminded of the love and compassion God has for me, it allows me to have compassion towards others even in the midst of adversity. I mean, how can you truly change your perspective, if you do not have compassion towards yourself? In order to truly change, you must first recognize the lack of compassion you have towards yourself. After you take that step, you must begin working towards self-love.

Self-Reflection

While sitting on my couch in the living room, I often reflect on how God has always been there for me-- even, at times that I had given up on myself, and worst of all, I had given up on God. You know, it's like the old saying: "You can't help others until you start helping yourself." Well, that is absolutely true. Oftentimes, we as humans are so quick to offer advice or our opinions to others as if we are the ones who are making the calls and walking in their shoes. Then we have the audacity to get mad and pass judgement on the person if they don't take heed to the advice that we give them. Look, let's be honest here… we all know of one, or maybe two people who are guilty of this. Heck, it may even be us.

Well, my friends, that is not the best road to travel. We have to be mindful of our approach in how we support those who are in need. We need to show compassion towards others. We can start by encouraging others, respecting others' views, and showing others kindness. There will be times when people shower us with compassion and other times when others have a lack of compassion and/or empathy towards us. However, we must continue to keep the light of compassion alive.

Compassion is the key to unlocking the insecurities, injustices, bias, and lack of knowledge that we, as people, inherently possess.

So, you may be wondering, what must I do to have the perspective to change? You must look within your heart. This requires you to set aside "Me Time" and reflect on the actions and reactions throughout life; and figure out why you do things the way you do or say the things you say. This is a tough process, but it is possible. It requires you to practice self-reflection to seek compassion within yourself without judgement. It is necessary to inspect oneself in order to truly live right by God and others.

We must love ourselves before we can truly love others without judgement. This requires you to understand that you come first. You must allow yourself the opportunity to grow and that may require you getting rid of toxic things and/or people! Once you have helped yourself then you will be ready to help them if their heart is open to receive it. This is often a hard concept for us to achieve. When we begin to love ourselves, we will be able to provide support and guidance to others. That is what compassion is all about.

Answering the Call

As an Assistant Principal in one of the largest urban school districts in the United States, I have seen and heard a lot. There have been many days and nights when I have yelled, cried, and asked myself why? Why did I decide to go into education? Why did God call me to do this work? The reality is, being an educator is draining, especially if you work with the demographics and/or population that is experiencing trauma, lack of resources, and poverty. The problem is significant.

- *Black and Latino families with children are more than 83% of inner-city youth. They report experiencing one or more traumatic events. (Michigan State University, College of Education, 2015).*
- *1 out of 10 children under the age of six living in a major American city report witnessing a shooting or stabbing. (Michigan State University, College of Education, 2015).*

The facts are there. Research studies prove that there is a correlation between poverty and trauma. However, although we know the facts, are we willing to make a change? Changing a system does not occur overnight and you must be willing to look at yourself to make that change. Let me give you an example.

Imagine that you are a health fitness expert or coach and you are trying to train a client on how to eat and live a healthier lifestyle, but you on the other hand are at Chick Fil A and Dairy Queen living your best life! The two cannot work and will not work. Did I hit home? Well, just think of other examples this statement could apply too… Hmmm…. I'll wait! When you are trying to change a system, and I mean truly, change a system, compassion is necessary. *Now stop! I mean now stop… Hold up… Wait a Minute. Now let me clear my throat!* We, as a community, must be willing to put in the hard work to change ourselves, our perspectives, and biases to create a systematic change.

You Are A System!

Let me define the word "system" for you.

> 1. a set of connected things or parts forming a complex whole, in particular. 2. A set of principles or procedures according to which something is done; an organized scheme or method (Webster's Dictionary,2019).

I truly believe that in order to change any system, you first have to look within oneself. You, my friend, are a system! Let's take this as an example: the human body operates as a system (legs, feet, eyes, arms, hands, and voice). You need all of these parts to function. But, what happens if you do not have one of these body parts? The answer is: You will not be able to operate the same or do the things you used to do. This reminds me of the time when I fractured my pinky toe. Nothing could have prepared me for what was about to happen.

Every year, me and my husband's family take a trip to the mountains of Gatlinburg, Tennessee. This is our time to bond, eat good food, tell stories, and to enjoy everyone's company. On this particular occasion, I was really looking forward to the trip because we were planning to go white water rafting. This was something on my bucket list and it was the season for it, so I thought. The night before the trip, the kids and I were out running a few errands. We were all filled with excitement and eagerly ready to get home to pack for the trip. Well, when we pulled up at our house, I remembered that I needed to take out the trash. So, I told my daughter Emerald, "Watch Braxton while I run in the house to get the trash to take out."

When I came out the door with the trash, I ran into a spider web, saw a spider, and immediately panicked.

I started swinging the trash bag into the spider web, but as I fought that spider, I rolled my right ankle causing bruises and a fractured toe.

Man was I upset and hurt. I felt every emotion that was out there. Now, I wasn't able to go white water rafting as planned. I could barely walk without pain. When my husband came home the following morning, I shared with him what happened and showed him my bruises. Of course, he handled the information well, due to him being a firefighter. But me, Angel Marie, on the other hand, was not fine and tried to make the best of it. I couldn't even put on my tennis shoes or any other type of sandal. All I could wear were a pair of $3.00 flip-flops purchased from Target.

Before we hit the road, I ran to the local store and grabbed some bandages to wrap my poor pinky toe. But, that didn't work either. Every time I tried to wrap it, it just felt worse. Each time I took a step, it felt like I was walking on pins and needles. Plus, the bandage kept falling off every time I tried to walk. After a few attempts of putting the bandage back on, I left it abandoned and accepted that it would just heal on its own.

As I reflect on this experience of fracturing my toe, I realize the beauty behind this story. God wants us to take the bandages off the things in life that have been a hindrance and is holding us back from experiencing growth and change in our relationship with Him and with others.

When you truly change, you will have a sense of peace and purpose for your life. You are then able to breathe and heal naturally because you are operating in compassion. When you have a bandage over a wound, it can only cover and protect those bruises and scars. However, God wants us to take off the bandages, whatever they are (hurt, pain, and emotional distress) to heal. Why? Because, He has the ultimate display of compassion. He loves us so much and He wants us to experience life at its best. We cannot truly enjoy life in the way that it was intended to be without changing our mental perspectives. There are several barriers that can create a blockage on receiving self-lovey (lack of communication, lack of ownership, and fear of the unknown) just to name a few. You must remove the barriers in order to receive the blessings. You must love yourself before you can truly love others in the way that they need to be loved.

The display of compassion towards others requires us to have compassion for ourselves. How can we teach and expect to show compassion to others, but fail to have compassion towards ourselves and family? It must start at home. It must start within oneself. So, you may be asking, how can I practice self-love? Well, I am glad that you asked! Here are a few things you can do to start practicing compassion towards yourself.

Me Time

I would like to call this "Me Time." Take 10-30 minutes out of your day for yourself and focus on relaxing. This can come in the form of practicing mindfulness, prayer, meditation, exercising, art making, and/or writing.

I enjoy going outside! There is beauty and healing in nature. God has placed many beautiful things on this Earth for us to receive His healing power. One of my favorite things to do is to exercise! Yes, I said it! Exercise. There are several things you can do. Even if that means going on a short walk, riding a bike, or practicing yoga. But, do it alone. When you put into practice your self-love routine, you will begin to see a shift in your mindset. This will allow you to love yourself even more because you will let go of those bandages that were not allowing you to heal and breathe in its natural state. I am a firm believer that there is power in "Me Time."

Now, I know some of you may say, "Well what about getting my nails done, going to the hair salon, and going to lunch with a friend?" It is not the same. Time to oneself helps encourage reflection and inner growth. Sometimes, we become so consumed by our daily to-do-list that we forget to just live! There is power in just being. There is power in just being still. There is power in being still in the moment! Recognize those peaceful moments that God has allowed in your life and take advantage of that time.

One of the most important people in my life is my Momma, and she taught me how to take advantage of my time and use it wisely. When she comes home, she turns off all electronics including her cell phone, computer, and she rests. Take my Momma's advice, this mindful exercise helps declutter your mind. It prevents you from getting trapped by social media, work, deadlines, money, friends, and family. Power down in order to power up for those who need you the most.

When you start practicing and showing compassion towards yourself, your value of self or your self-worth will increase for you to live the best life that you deserve. You will no longer settle for less because you will expect the best from yourself and others. My friends, I like to call this "The Mind Shift" aka "The Growth Mindset."

Growth Mindset

"In a growth mindset, people believe that their most basic abilities can be developed through dedication and hard work— brains and talent are just the starting point. This view creates a love of learning and a resilience that is essential for great accomplishment." (Dweck, 2015)

When you want to change and believe that you have the capacity to change, that will create a spark. This spark will create an enlightenment of various sensations in your mind to generate change. You will then begin to do research and put into practice the mindset that you want in order to grow and change for the better. During this time, you will start to have some wins. You will also notice that you are moving into a more positive space. You are dedicating yourself to the mindset to grow and to become an exceptional person.

When you operate in "The Growth Mindset" realm, you no longer have time for self-doubt and self-hate. You are too busy growing in love for oneself and others. For you to love others, you have to love yourself. That goes back to the concept of you having compassion towards yourself and setting aside "Me Time." You, then, begin to take care of home first. When you are secure in your house, it allows you to have a sense of purpose and meaning. You then can connect with others. Your sense of security reminds you of the good in the world and reassures your belief in God. When you are doing this, you are handling business in your house (your mind, heart and spirit) instead of trying to fix everyone else's house.

Now, I know that may be a tough pill to swallow for some, because some of us are natural helpers and some of us are practicing *nositritican* (meaning we know what's going on in our neighbor's house, but we do not know what's happening in our own house), so we constantly have our nose in someone else's house. Often, we are so consumed by what others are doing or not doing and it allows us to become stagnant in our personal growth. Instead of focusing on what others are doing or accomplishing, we must focus on our journey. That requires a lot of commitment and patience. Therefore, it requires you to spend time with yourself and God. I like to call this a personal relationship (PR).

Personal Relationship (PR)

I like to tell people that having a PR allows for you to communicate with God. When you have a PR, you are allowing the Holy Spirit to guide you with making decisions. It also provides opportunities for you to change and promotes growth within yourself. When you have a PR, the Holy Spirit is able to use you to communicate with others about the goodness of Jesus Christ, and most importantly, you are able to show unconditional love to others. Think about it. How can you grow and want to be there for others if you have never spent time alone? You need to practice this, so you can reflect on who you are as a woman or man of God. It is crucial to not only have faith in God, but to believe in yourself. Having a PR is critical to your growth! You must activate compassion towards yourself and your journey. When you have a PR, you will understand more of what it means to truly have compassion.

Compassion is also linked to grace. The word grace alone is a powerful word! When I think of grace, I immediately think of Jesus, and how He has adequately, without a shadow of doubt continued to pour out His grace upon me and my family. Like the rapper Big Sean references, I have "blessings on blessings on blessings!"

Many of the blessings I have received are simply because the Man above has opened them up for me. I like to think of grace and compassion as brothers and sisters. They are in the same family and provide many of the same benefits if we are operating in them regardless of our daily situations and interactions with others. Yes, we produce interactions with one another, and depending on how we deliver those interactions can determine the product that we are selling. This is why tone of voice is so important.

When I have a general conversation with adults about the power of relationships, I remind them that tone speaks volumes. As an educator, I sometimes hear my colleagues use sarcastic and stressful tones to ask students to do something. However, when the student uses the same tone, the teacher gets upset. I must admit that I, too, have used the sarcastic and stress tone (SST) as an educator and parent. However, it was not conducive at all. The student either:

    a) used it back with me
    b) did what I asked them to do, but took it out on another student, or
    c) did not complete the task/product at all.

Now, you as an adult have exhausted valuable time and energy into producing a product and you have nothing to show from it but bitterness, exhaustion, and hunger pains.

Ewwww! Ouch! Did I say that? Yes! Some of us are stressful eaters and when we create negative stress that is unnecessary, it transforms our thought process. We cannot indulge in unhealthy habits to release stress. We must dig deep in our hearts and hold on to faith. We must trust and believe that God will give us the wisdom to make change, but it requires action.

Operation Faith

What is hope? When you have hope, you trust and believe that the change will happen. I would like to say that this, my friends is operating in the faith realm. When you incorporate compassion towards change, God will give you hope. This requires you to pray. When you pray, you will begin to see a change in your perspectives that will allow you to praise God. I like to call this the three P's (Prayer, Perspective, and Praise). Now, let's take this a little further.

Faith is trusting and having confidence in God that what He said He would do, He will bring it to pass. Faith is not merely a word. It is an action.

When you truly have compassion towards change, you will begin to actively identify that type of change. It requires you to get out there and do some research. You will begin to pick up a book, listen to a podcast, and have life-changing conversations with like-minded people. Simply put, you will seek out the knowledge that you want to receive in order to change. It is that ol' saying you have to put something in to get something out.

When you take the first step of acknowledging the compassion that God has given you to change, you are taking the first step toward change. Throughout this enlightenment of having more compassion, you will begin to notice a shift within yourself. I like to call this a win. A win is also a miracle. Every win rather small or big is just that— a win.

When we wake up, it is a miracle! It is a day for us to get out there in this journey called life and help someone. It is an opportunity for us to achieve greatness and to let go of the hardship from yesterday. You have to let go of past guilt, upsets, setbacks, and trust that God is doing something new. He is about to bless you with an Ace card. The Ace card is ranked as the highest playing card in its suit while playing spades. Trust and believe that God is blessing you with an ACE (Advancements, Creativity and Experiences).

Think about someone you admire, or a business that you follow. Do you think those individuals gave up every time someone told them no, or when a door did not open at the time they wanted? No, they continued to push. They continued to let their compassion push them towards their dreams. They knew that God had called them to something greater than what their current circumstances were.

I am a firm believer that when filled with compassion, God will allow for you to experience peace when you are hit with storms and when the world may say no. I am a firm believer that God will provide healing when the world may say that this may be hard for you and you should give up. I am a firm believer that God will restore you when the world may say you are not strong enough. Friends, if we continue to allow what the world says, or others say determine our worth and our greatness, we are not living. We are not living out what God has called us to do.

Don't let anyone take your drive towards wanting to change for the better. When you are trying to follow your dreams, it requires change. I will repeat, it requires you to change. Sometimes, that may mean that you are giving up things and people who you never thought you would, in order for you to win.

Ask, Seek and Knock

Before I had my daughter Emerald, I was completely lost in self-doubt and self-worth. I never knew what it truly meant to love yourself and love someone else. I struggled with self-love and low self-esteem, because I didn't know my worth which led me to unhealthy relationships that deprived me mentally, emotionally, and spiritually. It wasn't until I became pregnant with Emerald, that I began to consistently seek God with the hopes that my life would change for the better. When I consistently sought God, He began to speak in my spirit and show me some things that I was not ready for. Believe me when you pray, and you are earnestly seeking God, be ready for Him to show you the truth. There were three areas that I focused on:

- 7 day fast
- The establishment of a prayer closet
- Read the Bible daily

    I was not ready for divorce, but I knew that there were some changes that I had to make so I could live a happier life and to do what was best for me and my daughter. It was my first time being married and disliked that I had to get a divorce. But, it was what was best for our marriage. This was one of the toughest experiences that I had to go through, but God was with me every step of the way. Although it was a painful experience, I knew a change needed to occur. We were both unhappy and the marriage was not healthy. I had to purse my happiness and worth.

    Since the divorce, the growth and wisdom that I have gained has helped others while they were going through relationship struggles with their marriage partner. Even though I had gone through this and was healing. I was still suffering from pain and I knew there was something else that I needed to address in order for true change to come about. Look, just because you feel like you have healed in one aspect of life, does not mean that you are completely healed. Healing is a process and a journey within itself. This meant I would have to self-reflect. I knew that I wanted to be married and that God had a husband for me, but I knew there was some growth that I needed to undergo in order to do so. I wanted my next marriage to be right and I wanted it to be a God thing.

    During prayer time, I told God what was on my heart and in my spirit (note I had been divorced for quite some time now) and how I had the desire to marry again, but for the right reasons. I then heard from God who then told me that I must continue to work on myself and read. He informed me to go to the bookstore and there I would find a book that would help me. I then got off my couch and immediately went to the bookstore.

When I entered the bookstore, I immediately felt a peaceful presence. I knew that this was where God was leading me to. I went over to the Christian genre book section and there it was, Robin Jones Gunn and Tricia Goye's "Praying for Your Future Husband: Preparing Your Heart for His" (2011). I picked up the book and read the summary on the back cover. The book focused on how prayer is key to unlocking the love story within your heart. The author's testimony guides you to pray for your future husband and with God, who is the lover of your soul.

This book would give me the opportunity to pray for myself, but also my future husband. It would also allow me to prepare my heart for growth and change.
I knew that this book was the one. As soon as I got back home, I immediately started reading the book. I finished the book within one week. I was excited about the wisdom I had received.

Slid In Ya DM's

After reading the book, I put into practice the information that I read and before I knew it, on the weekend of my birthday, I posted a picture on Facebook, and all of a sudden, Brandon slid in my direct messaging (DM). Now pause... before you get any ideas, it was not like that. Yet! I knew Brandon for quite some time now. We had both worked together at the Marriott Hotel when we were in our early twenties, still in undergrad. I was a hostess for one of the restaurants in the hotel and Brandon was a bellman. We always talked as friends and cracked jokes at work, but, we never took it any further. At the time, he had a girl, and I was in a relationship too.

However, despite the reality of it all, I couldn't help but think to myself as I watched him… that it was something in me that said I would love to marry him, while something else inside of me thought that would never happen. I didn't even think that he found me attractive. Well, boy was I wrong.

After messaging each other back and forth and catching up with each other, we decided to go out. Ladies, I would not call this a date. It was more like a meet and greet. This is a time when you are trying to get an understanding of who a man is and see if there is more than what meets the eye. However, I knew Brandon, but not on this type of level until we officially started dating. After a year of dating, we were engaged.

We both loved each other and the level of respect, compassion, and trust that he had showed me was undeniable. I never imagined that the seed I planted in my heart years ago would grow and blossom into something magnificent. By me taking this step of faith, it opened up two doors. First, it required me to learn. Second, it required me to grow in many areas. In order for me to sustain growth, I knew I had to communicate with my husband on many levels and that was new to me. But, it would certainly allow for the process of healing to begin. Why? Because, my husband loved me so much and knew that there was something behind my insecurities, which had, been buried in my past.

Chapter 2

Communication

"Communication leads to community, that is, to understanding, intimacy and mutual valuing." -Rollo May

    Being the oldest sibling requires you to be the responsible one, so I have learned. "Angel, here is some money for you and George to take with you to the store," said Momma. She would sometimes drop me and my brother off over our cousin's house. After my mom left, I always counted the money. I would count the money and tell my brother "We only have $3.00, so we better know what we're getting at the store." After me telling him that a few times he got the picture, after all I am the big sister.

    Me, my brother, and two cousins would walk to Winn Dixie to buy two Faygo pops and Totino's pepperoni pizza. My brother would have the leftover change and buy himself a Reese's. This was our drill, and everyone knew what we were buying and how much we were spending. Why? Because, this was communicated before we left the house. Even now, I sometimes find myself telling my kids what we're getting at the store and if they are allowed to buy something. This was just how I was raised and I'm grateful for that because it taught me the importance of buying only what you need.

    However, when it came to me effectively communicating with my parents about issues and pain that I was experiencing as a child it was very difficult for me. When I look back now, it's because I felt if I told my parents what I was dealing with or what had happened to me then my parents wouldn't love me or think that it was my fault. Even though now at the age of 33 I know that it was just a trick of the enemy. I was just a child and I didn't deserve mistreatment.

When I was in the third grade it was very challenging and a world wind. At times I felt lost and uncertain of life. I was molested by a family member. Not only did I deal with that, but I had lost my uncle Travis. He was my favorite uncle and he always made me feel safe. Even when he came to town from college at Fisk University; when he graduated and moved to New York City to become an English teacher he always made time for his niece Angel. He always talked to me about education and how important it is to know my history.

I have this one particular memory; he was visiting for the summer. We were sitting down in my grandmother's living room and he said are you ready to go to the mall! He knew I was ready, that was one of our favorite things to do. We got in my grandmother's Volvo and headed to Bashford Manor Mall. Man, those were the good ole' days. Inside of the mall we walked around and then we went to Walgreens. He said, "Angel, you can get all the candy you want." I walked around and me being me, I only got two kinds of candy. I got a Zero Bar and Gummy Bears. Even now, when someone offers something for me, I do not go overboard. I always get the minimal.

After walking out of Walgreens, we then went to a well-known clothing store called Bacon's (it is equal to a Dillard's or Macy's) to look around and then we hit up my favorite place in the mall. Sbarro's pizza!!! Anyone who knows me knows that I am a pizza lover and practically anything Italian lol. After I ate my slice of pizza we then got back in the Volvo and headed over to my uncle's lady friend's house. While on the road, my uncle loved to play this game. Whenever you are getting close to a red light and you are about to stop, you slowly hit your brakes then release, slowly hit your brakes then release, and it would create a motion in the car as if you were riding a ride!!! I absolutely loved it.

Not only did I enjoy us playing the game, but I remember us always listening to Sade or Prince. To this day, I still listen to Sade and when I listen to her music it warms my heart and brings a smile to my face. The tone of her voice puts me at ease and the cadence empowers me to keep believing. Her music is inspiring. There is something powerful in listening to music. Music is healing, and it is definitely a gift from God.

I can also think of times when my uncle would have a trip for underprivileged high school students in New York to go on a Historically Black College University (HBCU)'s tour in the south. He was always giving back and doing it with a smile.

My uncle always communicated with me and he always showed me unconditional love. Because of the seed he planted, it inspired me to pursue education as a profession. So, when he died unexpectedly, my heart was in pain. I was in the hospital and I remember touching his feet. I said to myself, these are the feet of a man who walked for a purpose.

After my uncle had died, another family member died at a young age. So, now I had two deaths in my family. To make matters worse, I was being molested and when I went to school, I was talked down to.

My third-grade teacher told me that I was "not smart" and that I was "dumb." Instead of trying to build a positive relationship with me and help me grow as a little person, she tore me down. She tore me down all the way to the core. To make matters worse… she was a black female. I tell people all of the time, just because a person may look like you, that does not mean they are for you! I was experiencing so much trauma that I was not able to concentrate on my learning. The teacher did not take the time to understand not only that I was dealing with trauma, but that my family had just moved from Louisville, Kentucky to our new home town in Jeffersonville, Indiana.

I felt pain and discouragement. This was very difficult as a child to process at such a young age. I didn't understand why this was happening. All I can remember that this was not a good feeling and I didn't know what to do.

The Call

By the end of my third-grade year, the principal called my mother. I remember it like it was yesterday. We were in our bedroom. I was sitting on the floor and my mother was sitting on the bottom bunk that I shared with my brother. She said Angel that was your principal. I said yes ma'am. She said he said that your grades are not good, and you are behind in your reading. He is suggesting that we hold you back a year. I was so upset. I was so ashamed. I felt so dumb. I felt guilt. I felt that it was all my fault.

Instead of me communicating with my mom right at that moment, I couldn't. I did not know how to. As I sit right now at the hair salon watching my daughter get her hair done, I still see that scene. I still hear those words. I still remember those feelings. I still see how I was sitting on the floor. After sitting on that floor for some time. I had to figure out what I was going to do next. How was I a third grader going to deal with being ridiculed at school, it was already bad when my teacher told me I was dumb. I had no choice, but to deal with it.

The first day of third grade for the second time. Let me take a deep breath. All I can remember was me going to the cafeteria for breakfast. The cafeteria was the spot, wait let me stop there. The cafeteria is still the spot for you to see what is going on and to be seen. Believe me, I know. I am an educator! After I got my breakfast, I sat down at the table with my friends. Then a teacher approached me and said Angel you need to go sit at that table over there. It was nearly two tables over from where I was sitting. I then asked her why? She said that is where the third graders sit. My heart dropped. When I sat down, I was embarrassed even more. People then started asking me why I was sitting over there, and they were pointing at me.

All Stakeholders

Thank goodness for the school custodian, Mr. Roberts. He came over and spoke to me and helped ease my pain. From that day forward, I started to feel better. I would see Mr. Roberts every other Friday at Pizza Hut (his second job) so I could turn in my paper for BOOK IT! BOOK IT! is a reading initiative that motivates students to read more books. Each student would have a goal (number of books to read) and when they met their goal, they would receive a certificate for a free personal pan pizza. It's that simple. Mr. Robert's would always greet me with a smile and was very positive.

As each day passed, I began to make new friends, I learned more about myself and I discovered my gift in playing sports. Playing basketball was my outlet, running track was my outlet, cheerleading was my outlet, and dancing was my outlet. Me being involved in after school activities helped me to bury the pain, but deep down inside I was still just a child who was not comfortable to communicate with my parents what I was feeling and what was going on.

Years went by and I continued to focus my energy into sports and after school activities. During my seventh-grade year, my school counselor had signed me up for a class called *Exploration*. When I entered the classroom, there were only seven of us, not including the teacher. As I sat down at the front of the classroom, Mr. Byer's gave the syllabi to the class and told us that we would be reading several novels, having authentic discussions, and then take a test. To make a long story short, this was a Black History Literature class and it was taught by a white male.

To my surprise, Mr. Byer's opened my mind to reading and I had a newfound love of books and literature. After my first week of class, I asked my parents if I could have a desk, so I could read and study. And, before I knew it, my parents bought me a desk where I could do my homework and stay up until the late hours reading books and studying for tests. The desk was white with black trimming. It came with a black lamp and three shelves at the bottom to store my books and folders. This desk was immaculate! Me being able to house all of my books in one location was incredible. I enjoyed learning, it was my outlet. It allowed me to challenge myself and I grew so much from it. Me being able to learn and understand was amazing.

This was the first time ever that I felt smart. This was the first time ever that I knew a teacher believed in me and encouraged me to learn. This was the first time ever that a teacher did not look at me as just the "black girl" or "a black girl" but as a student who was thirsty for knowledge. I was finally valued as a student. Due to Mr. Byers valuing me as a student and my parents being my biggest supporters, it helped me to further my education. I began taking college preparatory classes in high school and completed my doctoral degree. Those negative seeds did not discourage me from having the love of learning.

Positive Relationships

As an Assistant Principal, I tell our teachers all of the time when I am conferencing with them, it is all about building and sustaining a positive relationship. When a student knows and feels that you believe and care about them, they will show up each and every day ready to learn.

Ready to be their best. Ready to do their best. Ready to give their best. Students can tell when you are being real and truly care about them as an individual. Remember we were all once young and students ourselves.

Due to my uncle planting the seed of knowledge and now, Mr. Byer's providing water to that seed, I was able to see the sunlight to help me grow as a student. This was a pivotal moment in my education experience. My family valued education however, when both parents and educators value a child's education, that makes a world of a difference in the life of the student.

Teachers can be outlets for students if they self-reflect. Often times I have been around educators who think of themselves as "all-knowing" due to the degree(s) and/or who they know. They are so quick to pass judgement on others without giving people the benefit of the doubt. They think that they have never had any hard days or any negative experiences— that their childhood was perfect. Regardless of how these teachers may appear, they have some areas of growth and they have struggles. Believe it or not, often times they are passing bias and it is creating a climate and culture that is not beneficial for all stakeholders.

I have been in the field of education for 12 years and I always can tell the real from the fake. I can tell when a teacher is really there for the students or just there for the summers, checks, and flexibility. It is a shame that there are a number of teachers who do not want to teach students in various demographics and if they do decide to teach, they have the mentality of "I am going to come and save this black child…" That is why it is so important for when you are trying to truly change a mindset; you have to understand the community in which you are trying to change. It really starts with communication.

Communication = Powerful Community

When I think of the word communication, the word community immediately comes to mind. You can't have communication without a community. Now, I know some of you might be thinking Angel I talk to myself, "yes dear that may be true," but do you answer yourself? If the question is yes, then that is a whole different topic that we will discuss at another time at a later date. Often times people do not effectively communicate what they want and what they need to get the job done.

I believe it's not just about communicating to others about the issues, but we must make and create sound action that will help bring about change. Then you will begin to create a systematic change. Schools will be able to sustain a positive culture and climate. All members of the school community will be valued and treated equitable. Yes, this will take some time due to our histories pass.

You have to plan out that change, if things happen to derail the plan, no worries. Go back to your manuscript, adjust, and get back out there. Don't let others write your story for you. Don't allow others to dictate what God has given to you. We are a gift and if we utilize our gift in a productive way, it can create opportunities for others to change. Why? Because, you communicated. I have learned that when you take the time to truly communicate with others, God will use you to help bring about change, but it can also allow for others to grow more in their walk with Christ. I am a witness of this.

By taking the first step of communicating with my husband about my past, I was able to start the process of healing. He was there every time with an open heart and ear, willing to listen to his wife pour out her heart and pain through tears and actions. Every time, he listened without judgement, offered advice to help me, and encouraged me to pray and seek more. When I prayed God would remind me that my past will help me in my future and that He is always with me. He taught me forgiveness, gave me peace, and reminded me that I have a future. This statement just reminds me of the time I visited the bank.

After successfully completing my first year as an Assistant Principal, I was looking forward to resting at home where I wasn't required to check emails for an entire month-- I will explain my theory about emails later. All I could think about was getting home, spending time with my kids, and catching up on all my favorite T.V. shows, but first I had to stop by the bank to pay our mortgage. When I walked in the bank, there was a long line with only two tellers. After waiting for 15 minutes, I could tell that one of the tellers was new due to the look of distress on her face.

"Can I help you?" asked the teller.

"How are you?" I responded. "I need to make a mortgage payment and I don't have my account number, but I need you to look it up."

After running my transaction that took a couple of minutes, it was apparent that she made a mistake and the Assistant Manager was called.

"What's going?" she asked.

The teller stated, "I messed the transaction up again."

The Assistant Manager did not hesitate at all with showing her how to reverse the transaction.

"If you need anything else, let me know," she said before returning to help her customers.

I could tell that the teller was over it and frustrated. So, I kindly asked her with a smile, "How long have you been working here?"

"It's my first week on line," she whispered.

My smile grew bigger. "You are doing a good job," I reassured her. "It will get better."

I knew exactly how she felt. At one time, I was in her shoes.

"When I was in undergrad, I worked for the exact same bank and had the exact same position," I confided in the teller.

She smiled, holding back tears as I reaffirmed and encouraged her to have a good day.

As I walked away, I could hear God's voice and word clearly, reminding me to:

> "Be strong and courageous. Do not be afraid or terrified because of them, for the Lord your God goes with you; he will never leave you nor forsake you." Deuteronomy 31:6 (NIV)

I began to have tears of joy, because I remember being in her shoes (working two jobs, being on line with my sorority, and being a youth minister) and telling myself that one day I will be an Assistant Principal. God had put that in my spirit. God had aligned us two to have a joyful encounter to remind us that God is real, and God keeps His promises. Thank God for communication. Thank God for community.

Just think, if I was too proud to share my story with that young woman, she wouldn't have been able to receive the encouragement and I wouldn't have been able to receive the joy of perseverance. I tell you, there is power in knowing that God has your back and even when you don't see it and it comes to pass, brings you so much joy and peace. It is an amazing feeling.

I have learned that in this journey called life, we all have stories and it is up to us to decide if and when we are going to share our story. You may think it's minimum or inadequate, but you never know what seeds you may have planted in that person's spirit. When we decide to stop holding back our stories, we will be able to receive unspeakable peace and joy like none other. I believe we will be able to stop generational curses from occurring. We will break the chains. In order to share your story, there are three things that you must do to start the process. I admit it will not be an easy one, but trust and believe it will be rewarding.

    1. Acknowledge that you do have a story.
    2. Ask God to help you heal and show you how to communicate with others about your story.
    3. Trust that God will provide the opportunity for you to share your story.

Sharing your story is taking the first step towards healing. However, you will need an individual(s) for you to collaborate with to help you to heal, grow and change for the better.

Chapter 3

Collaboration

"Along we can do so little; together we can do so much." – Helen Keller

Springtime and summer time-- that is all me. However, springtime is one of my absolute favorite seasons, and I would have to say that it's the same for the rest of our family. During the warm weather, I simply enjoy going outside, riding my bike at the waterfront, and playing in the park with my kids. Seeing their smiles and hearing their laughter brings me great joy. I could go on and on about how much I love being outside. Even hearing the booming sound from my husband's motorcycle engine that he starts in the driveway, excites me!

During these seasons, we as a family spend more time together outside, especially since our daughter is out of school and I am off for a month. This is the time that we take our family vacations. In order to successfully plan for those vacations, park outings, bike rides, and ice cream visits it does take collaboration amongst my husband and me. Now, I know some of you might say Angel, that is simple: how does it take collaboration?

Well, being happily married takes having open communication to have collaboration. Regardless of what relationship you may be in you have to have collaboration and it must be consistent. At times, I have planned something for our family and forgot to even communicate it with Brandon, to find out that he already had something planned or I forgot that he had to work overtime. At times, I have forgotten to tell my family about our daughter's upcoming events, informing them at the last minute. At other times, I have dropped the ball at work, due to me forgetting to inform my boss, and having so much on my plate.

Occasionally, I have dropped the ball on my friendships on not being there for them the way that I need to be, due to me running around taking care of other needs. The point is that we have all been guilty at one time or another for dropping the ball. It is necessary to drop the ball at times. Yes, I said it! It is necessary to drop the ball at times. Why? One, it reminds us that we are human, we make mistakes, and are imperfect. Second, it's important to realize that you will never be perfect, but it is okay to strive to do your best. Third, it allows you to focus on your areas of growth and learn how to do better next time. That is why collaboration is so essential for change and true growth. You cannot grow without collaboration.

A Helping Hand

Having collaboration is necessary for changing a system. When you are trying to change a system, you are going to need various stakeholders to do so. God has blessed you with an individual(s) who can help you on your journey. You cannot do it alone. Regardless if you think you are educated enough, strong enough, financially enough, the bottom line is you are not. God did not design us to be out here in this world alone and to do things without receiving the help and wisdom from others. That last sentence reminds me of when I was going through a divorce and I was a single mother. If anyone has gone through a divorce, all can attest there is no such thing as an easy divorce. Divorce is hard, and it forces you to learn and grow to make you a better person, that is if you choose to do so.

Often times, society and especially those who are religious (that is a topic that we will discuss later), look at divorce as a bad thing. When I was going through my divorce people passed judgement and was so quick to give me their opinions as if they were walking in my shoes. For some reason, people looked at me with shame and disappointment. It wasn't until I finally stood up for myself and said this is my journey. When I started telling close relatives, friends and church members, they finally got the point, because it was in the tone in which I said it. I knew that it would be a tough transition for me and my daughter. I knew that I would need some help, because I was a hard-working mother. I worked full time as a teacher, ECE (Exceptional Child Education) department chair, Youth minister, was in school full time working on my doctoral degree, and most importantly, I was raising my daughter Emerald who was just two years old at the time.

    While seeking God in prayer, it was placed in my spirit that it was time for me to ask my parents if I could move back home with them. I was like heck no! But, then God shared with me that this would not be permanent but just for a year. This was a tough pill for me to swallow because I am a very independent woman. I do not, I repeat, I do not like depending on or asking anyone for anything. I cannot even think of the last time I ever borrowed money from anyone (maybe high school). I prided myself on that. So, for me having to ask my parents if I could come back home was tough. I had to set aside my feelings and my pride to do what was in the best interest for me, but more importantly my daughter.

    After finishing the phone call with my parents, I felt relieved. They were excited to have us home and wanted to help me get through this tough experience. It took some time for me to get used to being back home. While I lived with my parents, it took a lot of collaboration on everyone's part. My parents stepped in to help pick up the pieces and reminded me that this too shall pass. My parents knew that I was hurting, and they did their best in comforting me and showering me with love.

    But, I will tell you this. Regardless of who walks out of your life, your parents or loved ones cannot and will not fill that void. The only one who can truly heal you from the pain is the one above. This experience had me fall right on my knees even more in prayer and seek His will for my life. Once I accepted what it was. God started healing me. It took me years to be free and heal from the wounds. But, God! Since I received helped from my parents, it allowed for me to continue to work, complete my doctoral degree, and reflect more on what I really wanted for my life. I knew my time at their house would require some true collaboration.

    The word collaboration is defined as the action of working with someone to produce or create something. My parents came with open arms with this process. I communicated with them my goals as to paying off medical bills that I had at the time, saving money, and buying my first home within a year. These were healthy goals, but I knew that I could and would accomplish them. I would have to understand my resilience in the midst of growth. I would be growing spiritually, mentally, financially, and how could I forget physically. I was definitely committed to getting my snap back for sure. As a result of me showing my parents I had compassion for change, it allowed for me to effectively collaborate and communicate with them. I knew if I continued to be consistent about this change then this would help our community (home and family).

    By living with my parents at an older age, it allowed for me to see my parents' marriage in a more profound way. When you are married, every individual has their role to play. Every person has their strengths and areas of growth. When you realize that and communicate about it, the family as a whole is able to function for the best. Seeing my parents operate the way they do allowed for me to open up to them about some of the pain I had experienced.

    But, it wasn't until I had married Brandon, when I was able to fully communicate with my parents about my trauma and how I was healing from it. My parents listened and comforted me. They knew I just wanted an ear and a safe space to share. Yes, it was tough. I was not sure how it was going to be taken. I knew God was with me and my husband was right there sitting next to me. My family showed me not only with their words, but with their actions that they were committed to my healing journey. They took the time to listen and allowed for me to vent without judgement.

Chapter 4

Commitment

"Productivity is never an accident. It is always the result of a commitment to excellence, intelligence, planning, and focused effort." – Paul J. Meyer

August 14, 2016 was a day that I will always remember. I had been waiting on this moment my entire life and I was READY! I was ready spiritually, emotionally and physically. I mean, no one can prepare you for this major step and no one can tell you how it's truly going to be and what to expect. Why? Because, everyone has a different journey and we all have different perspectives on how we process life changing moments in our lives. No matter how many times you may have done it, when you KNOW this is the moment and KNOW this is the one and you have ZERO doubts, it is the most precious and sacred peace ever! This my friends I am talking about marriage.

Usually, when people say the word *commitment* they automatically think of marriage. Why? Because marriage is something that God has ordained since the beginning of time. Now, I absolutely agree that society has not upheld marriage in the same way in the early years and that is due to many issues both positive and negative. Some people believe that a marriage certificate is just a piece of paper. Some believe that marriage is about being with someone who makes you happy. While others believe that marriage is about acquiring financial security. Regardless of what your opinion may be, marriage is something that is sacred and requires *commitment*.

When people also use the word *commitment* they say I am committed to my relationships, my family, my friends, and my kids. All of these things are forms of *commitment* and one is not greater than the other, but first I would like to think that when the word *commitment* comes into a conversation, we should first be committed to Christ. Doing God's work! That is hard for some to do, I believe it! I was once that person who felt that I had to take care of others first, myself, and then God. When you first take care of yourself (meaning being intentional about taking time out for spiritual and mental growth), you will discover that you are being committed to God and the work that He has called you to do. Both are interchangeable.

By reading His word, listening to His word and Praying about His word (about what you read), can have a positive impact not only in your life, but it will help transform you into becoming a better you. In fact, my friends, if I can be so ever frank that is what we as humans are trying to do. Think about it for a minute. The moments we spend at the gym, eating healthy, keeping up with our image (hair, nails clothes... well that was for the ladies), reading books, obtaining a degree, landing that job, and or career that you have always wanted, and the list goes on.

We are striving to become a better YOU! Friends, that is nothing wrong at all in doing that, but in the process, who are you doing it for? Are you going to dedicate and use your gifts, talents and blessings you received to help others? I mean really, are you? Are you going to give back to your family, your community the youth? I mean how are you going to do so? I know it's tough! I know it's a lot and you may say, Angel you are asking a lot! Really, I am asking a lot! I disagree, I am a firm believer it starts in your home. With those who are closest to you. Building those positive relationships. Showing your family that you care, showing up when it means others aren't.

Rarely, this does not happen in our communities that are stricken with poverty and it was systematically set up that way, especially for our black communities. Now, let me pause. I know someone who is not a minority and or black is like why did she say "our"? I am glad you asked. Regardless of where you live, what race, ethnicity, socioeconomic class, religion and etc. we are all affected by poverty. Due to systematic and social injustices in the past some communities were and have been stripped of their businesses, schools and safety and it has caused generations upon generations of not being able to produce their best!

The time is now that communities come together to stand and do what is just. Yes, trauma has taken place, discomfort has taken place, injustice has taken place, but because it happened in the past does not mean it is going to happen with you. No way! No way! It is time to put a stamp on that past and mail it back to the past! Just because your mother lived in poverty doesn't mean you have to.

Just because your family is overweight and dealing with health issues doesn't mean you have to. Just because your dad is uneducated doesn't mean you have to. Just because your mom or dad is incarcerated doesn't mean you have to. Just because you were raised by your granny doesn't mean that you won't take care of your kids!

The time is now! Stop living in the past and be committed to now! Be committed to your future! Be committed to God and trusting that He knows what is best! Be committed to You being the best You! Meaning, do your part. Showing up and showing out in the gifts and talents that God has for You! Being true to the beauty of You! Being true to the man or woman of God who has called You to do great things! Knowing and trusting that change will come and it is due to the fact that you are committed to change.

You are not giving up on changing for the better. You are not settling for mediocrity. You are stretching for elevation! Elevation in your finances, elevation in your personal relationships, elevation in family, elevation in your career, elevation in your health… elevation… elevation… elevation… in your commitment to Christ!

Pussssh!!!

I often tell people that when you are trying to change a system, you will have some battle wounds. You will have some headaches, heart aches and pains. But, you have to stay committed. It is just like when you are in the process of getting healthy, you want to lose weight. Believe me that is a tough commitment. I have been there!!! I have two beautiful children and both pregnancies were not easy and they were different. When I was pregnant with Emerald I had morning sickness for two trimesters. I could only eat four items (watermelon, grilled cheese, Ramon noodles, and sausage and biscuit). My third trimester I was able to broaden my food palate which was needed.

During my first pregnancy, I prepared to have a natural birth. Me and my sorority sister had it all planned out. She had just had a baby not too long before me and gave me some great motherly advice. She informed me that no number of classes would prepare me for giving birth and that I would eventually learn that there are things in life that I can't control. Boy was she right! Preparing for a child makes you grow and requires you to see life in a different light.

Of course, my mother did too. But, like any woman who has experienced child labor, each child, every delivery, and every moment brings something new. I remember it like it was yesterday. In the morning, I started having lower pressure pain in my belly. I called my mom and she said Angel go to the hospital. Today is the day. So, we went to the hospital and they sent me back home. When I got back home the pain was intense and I was even in more pain. I called my mom again and she said Angel go back to the hospital and I am on my way to catch a flight back home.

When I arrived at the hospital, they put me in a room and kept a close watch on me and the baby. Before you knew it, Emerald's heartbeat was lowering, which we found out it was due to the umbilical cord being wrapped around her neck. They had to perform an emergency cesarean section (C-section). Thank God, my nurse had checked, and I was able to go into surgery immediately. Within two minutes of seeing the cord wrapped around her neck, I was given an epidural. While the needle was being placed in my back, I started to feel the pressure of Emerald and the doctor. I am blessed to say that on February 4, 2011, I received the greatest gift ever-- my healthy daughter Emerald. She is such a blessing and filled with so much love and personality. Her ability to learn and grow is phenomenal.

Six years later, July 19, 2017 I gave birth to Braxton. This pregnancy was a little bit different. I had three cysts the size of golf balls that caused severe pain and that required me to be hospitalized for a week. I ended up having a C-section and delivering a healthy baby boy. Needless to say, I was a parent committed to my children and I still continued to be. Being a parent is a tough job and you never how much of a responsibility you have until you are in it. It is a complete blessing.

By facing my trauma, it allowed me to be there for my children even more. It allowed for me to work on myself as an individual, so I could be the best version of me as possible. When I have questions or concerns pertaining to my children I take it to the Lord. I ask Him to order my steps and to give me the patience I need to raise them. Every time He has showed up and showed out for Emerald and Braxton. I asked God to teach me how to listen and train them up in the way they should go. There is power in the word of God. There is power in being committed to God by taking to Him our deepest fears and worries. Not only shall we be committed to growth and change, but we have to stay consistent in the journey of growth.

Chapter 5

Consistency

"Success isn't about greatness. It's about consistency. Consistent hard work leads to success. Greatness will come."- Dwayne Johnson

    You never really realize the harm that you have caused until it actually hits you. The truth of the matter is that often times we are dealing with past pain and trauma and we truly have not recognized how that pain has and is affecting our present. Trauma can most certainly shape our future as well. I have heard that our actions, consequences and experiences can shape us. But, I am going to challenge that. I believe it starts with our mind. Our thoughts can certainly shape our actions. Those thoughts could be positive or negative. When you are consistent with your thought process, it can shape your actions for the better.

    The relationships in my past were not healthy for me mentally, emotionally, spiritually, and physically (theses I like to consider my lifelines). I have been hurt in all four of the lifelines, but the one that I struggled the most was mentally. Why? Being mentally stable is a strength within itself and you have to be able to balance that with all of the categories. Your mind is a powerful tool to help unlock the worries, doubts and insecurities that clouds your perception of self. When your thoughts are not right then that will begin to transfer negative emotions into your heart and body. Those thoughts then can create a world of "what if's" and deter you from your true journey. You then begin to operate in your feelings and not operate in faith. When you are operating in your feelings, it can create a negative experience. Therefore, those experiences can create a hindrance in your ability to grow. At any point of time when something or someone attacks, your lifeline it can seriously cause damage in not only that area, but it can run over to another lifeline.

It takes me back to a song that my granny sings at my grandfather's church. I can see her sitting up on the choir stand with her enormous hat and her joyfully singing, smiling, and rocking back and forth.

> *"Walk with me Lord*
> *Walk with me*
> *Walk with me Lord*
> *Walk with me*
> *You walked with my mother, walk with me*
> *You walked with my father, walk with me*
> *Walk with me Lord, walk with me..."*

When I sing those lyrics of the hymn "Walk with me Lord," it does something inside my soul. It's like God gives me an extra boost of confidence, strength, and perseverance like none other to push through the circumstances and be resilient throughout it all. Knowing that my strength comes within. You can eat healthy all you want. You can exercise all you want. You can Namaste and Amen every day. But, if your spirit and mind is not centered and aligned with Jesus Christ you are going to walk around frustrated with life, frustrated with your circumstances, frustrated with people, frustrated with self, and frustrated with God. If you truly understand that this is not a feeling walk, but a faith walk then you will begin to trust in God's perfect timing! Resilience is something that you already have inside of you, but you have to activate it daily. Life is going to happen, disappointment is going to happen, and people will let you down. But, how are you going to react when it occurs?

Are you just gonna sit around and mope about it? Are you gonna talk and talk about it until you are tired of talking about it? Are you gonna compare your life to someone else? No. Heck no. You shouldn't, why? Because, God has created you in the image that is perfect for you. There is only one you. People may mimic, but there is only one you. That crooked smile, those long legs, short hair long hair don't care... all of those things make you YOU. When you begin to look at the true beauty inside of you, then you will begin to be confident in the person that God has called and created you to be. I have learned that you have to be consistent with God. You have to consistently seek God's face. There are three things that you can do to help activate your resilience.

    1. Activate your prayer life
    2. Activate your super power (Holy Spirit)
    3. Activate your Faith (remembering that this is a faith walk not a feelings walk)

This faith walk is not an easy one, but it is one that you must be consistent. Consistency is a word that we as humans throw around in various arenas and communities. Oftentimes, I feel people use the word, but don't truly value its meaning and what it can do for our lives when we truly utilize it.

According to dictionary.com it provides four definitions for the word consistency.
1. A degree of density, firmness, viscosity, etc.
2. Steadfast adherence to the same principles, course, form, etc.
3. Agreement, harmony, or compatibility, especially correspondence or uniformity among the parts of a complex thing.

4. The condition of covering or holding together and retaining form; solidarity or firmness.

Every definition for this word pertains to you not only having consistently in your life but sustaining it. It's great to start off with something that you love and want to accomplish. But, how many of us will stick with it when the road gets tough. When you are doubting yourself and doubting others. When you begin to doubt your journey, your calling, your gifts and talents, your dreams because it is getting hard. The truth of the matter is that we all have had our doubts, we have all doubted others, and we have even doubted God himself a time or two.

The power in knowing and trusting God is that he never has doubted us. He knows what we are capable of starting and finishing. That is why it is so vital that we sustain a personal relationship (PR) in Christ. We must remain consistent in our daily walk with Christ. Simply put (you must remain consistent in your daily walk with Christ). That statement along speaks many volumes, but how often do we really break down what it means? How often do we live by those words? How often do we meditate on those words? Let's dissect that statement.

You. That word means You. NOT your mom, dad, aunt, uncle, child, boss, co-worker, but You. That means that you must remain consistent. It is not up to your spouse, significant other or parent to be responsible for your relationship with Christ. Next, is the word consistent. In order to truly see change in your life you must consistently seek God on a daily to grow. Growth doesn't happen overnight, but it is a process. Think about the life cycle of a butterfly.

Transformation

We know that butterflies have a complete metamorphosis. But, this did not happen overnight. It had to go through four different stages that allowed for them to grow. Each stage was a test and it required them to grow and move on to the next stage until they had achieved their goal. The first stage is the egg- the egg is very small and is placed on a leaf of a plant. Every egg is unique and has various features. The egg shape depends on the type of butterfly that laid the egg.

The second stage is the larva or caterpillar- during this stage the caterpillars are feasting. When the egg hatches the caterpillar begins to eat the leaf that it was born onto. It eats its own leaf due to the mother butterfly needing to lay her eggs on that specific type of leaf. They are really specific to which leaf they lay their eggs on. When they are consuming food, they are doing it quickly, so they can grow and expand. Their exoskeleton (skin) does not stretch or grow so they then start the process of molting, which is the shedding of old skin. This process happens several times while the caterpillar is growing.

The third stage is pupa- this is a transitional period. This is the period when the caterpillar is done growing and they have reached their full weight and length. From the outside eye it may appear as if they are resting. But inside they are quickly changing. They are experiencing metamorphosis. They are becoming all the parts which make them a butterfly. The final stage-the adult butterfly. This is when the butterfly emerges from the third stage (chrysalis). The wings are folded against the body. This is due to the butterfly having to fit all of its new parts inside of the pupa.

These four stages are very similar to us as humans. We are placed on earth. We did not choose our parents and families. We did not choose what city, town and/or community we will be residing in. However, we do have a choice to decide if and when we are willing to embrace our lives and strive towards the best. Yes, when you are trying to change for the better there will be some challenging times.

There are going to be times when we will be in the larva-caterpillar stage when we are young and learning from those who are raising us. But, when you become of age it is time for you to start eating off your own leaves creating food for your family. Getting rid of the old in order to receive your wings of strength to provide for others and to share knowledge. It takes time when you are changing for the better. It takes consistency. Being mindful about the need for change for something better. You are trying to get your wings. Why? So, you can help yourself and then go back and help others. That is what I have noticed throughout my journey. Everyone that starts with you in the beginning will not be there to see you finish in the end and that is okay. Because, it is your daily journey.

Let's look at the word daily. Daily means daily. No if ands or buts. It's not weekly. It's not monthly but daily. Seek the presence of God when you are praying, driving, eating, and when you fellowship with others. God is around us. He is here. Right now, waiting on you to communicate with him about your thoughts and concerns. He wants to help, but often times we let sin and others dictate who God is to us. God is omnipresent. God is omnipotent. God is omniscient. Omnipotent-means He is all powerful. Omnipresent- means He is all present (He is everywhere). Omniscience-means He is all knowing. Do not and I repeat do not put ANY limitations on God. I have seen Him show up and show out in my life and others numerous times. So, trust that if He did it for me, He will definitely do it for you.

Last, but certainly not least, we must walk with Christ. Oftentimes, we walk and follow what others are doing. We have to start seeking God on our own terms for what He wants us to do on this journey called life. When you have experienced past trauma, I have learned that it is a daily process. You cannot and will not be healed overnight. It takes patience and prayer. You have to trust the process and allow God to share with you how you are going to be resilient in the process. Think about the trauma that has occurred in your life, it did not happen overnight, and it surely did not impact your thought process for just a short moment.

You must be consistent in your process of seeking change. You have to be reflective in your thoughts, actions and reactions. You must have consistent collaboration and communication with the Man above. You also have to have critical conversations with the ones you love that truly allow for you to have an open space without judgement. That or those individuals must understand that it is your journey and you have allowed for them to come into your space to share your deepest moments. Not all and I will repeat, not all people will be understanding of your journey. That is why you must be in prayer and reflect. You must ask God who is the individual(s) that can help you get through this. Sometimes it is a spouse, a parent, friend, therapist or counselor. Whoever they are you will know because God will show that to you. My person that I trust and can have an open space is my husband.

You Love Me

Brandon does an amazing job of allowing me to share with him my deepest thoughts and darkest moments without judgement. Before I married Brandon, I didn't realize the true meaning of having a healthy relationship. By me having a healthy relationship with him, required me to face my own insecurities and biases. He took the time to listen to me and allowed me the time to heal. Brandon provided me with a loving perspective and words of encouragement. Fireman Jackson is a man of action.

There would be moments when we would have discussions and I would just cry. My husband was patient with me and he still is. He provided me with a safe space and comforted me. I must admit, it took me a while to do that, because I first had to be willing to have several conversations with myself. I realized that in order for me to grow I had to be willing to reflect within myself. I knew I had to face my past, so I could receive the healing that I deserved. We all deserve to heal and experience joy in the midst of the process.

There would be times when I would go into my prayer closet and God would reveal something to me that I needed to hear. Then, as soon as I made my way back into the living room, Brandon would just speak of the same thing that God shared with me. I am a firm believer in the power of the Holy Spirit. God will put people in your life to help you grow and change for the better. You have to be open and willing to try.

Yes, this will be hard. It will be scary. Allow yourself to cry and be angry. It is okay to be angry and it's okay to cry. It is okay to have those emotions that you are feeling. It is okay to ask yourself why? Why me Lord? I am a firm believer that God allows for things to happen and He knows the outcome. We have to trust Him in the midst of growth. It is a tough thing to do when you have so much going on. When times are hard and there is no one to look to. I have been there, but I know that I can always stand on the word of the Lord. You have to have a solid foundation. My foundation is my faith. I cannot operate in my feelings, even though it is human for me to do so. I must operate in my faith. I must be willing to take a step back and go back to what I know and what has gotten me through all those tough times. It has been my faith.

Life will have its ups and downs. Money comes and goes. Time waits for no one. But, one thing that should never be taken away is your foundation. When you have a firm foundation, you can have joy throughout it all. Believe me, it is a process. This journey called life. Please don't think for one second that you will not be tested, because you will. I am reminded in His word of these two scriptures:

> Consider it pure joy, my brothers and sisters, whenever you face trials of many kinds, because you know that the testing of your faith produces perseverance. Let perseverance finish its work so that you may be mature and complete, not lacking anything. James 1:2-4 (NIV)

> Blessed is the one who perseveres under trial because, having stood the test, that person will receive the crown of life that the Lord has promised to those who love him. James 1:12 (NIV)

Yes, I know it may be hard, but you have to praise your way through. You have to pray your way through. You have to change your perspective throughout it all. The thing about change is that it is uncomfortable, and it will hurt. But, those growing pains will pass.
It's a feeling that is deep in your stomach that you can't shake because there is something in you that is pushing you towards healing. It is pushing you towards greatness.
When you are being consistent about change it will not be an easy journey. You will have to have those tough conversations or what I like to call (critical conversations)

CC's with yourself and others that may make you feel uneasy. But, you must trust the process. You must trust God to lead you every step of the way. He said in His word that He would never leave you nor forsake you. After I have had that critical conversation, a huge weight was lifted off my chest and I was relieved. There was no barrier at all. I had peace and understanding.

It is not enough to pray, but you must actively seek the Lord if you want to change. The first three letters of the word actively is ACT. You must take action to change. The process of change is all around you. It's in our daily actions, conversations, thoughts, and etc. This reminds me of the saying that my husband says the universe gives you the opportunities for you to change. Whatever you are wanting to work on the universe will put that in your face, so you can have the opportunity to change. That my friend is the process of growth and we can all use growth.

I have a secret that I would like to share with you all: this concept of the power of change is already inside of you. You decided to pick up this book and read it. Looking for change within yourself to better yourself. So, you can leave a legacy for your family. You know that there are some things that you need to change and grow from.

Understanding your resilience in the midst of growth is occurring as you read this book. You then will realize that God has already placed resilience in you, but it is up to you to activate it. It is up to you to walk in it. There were times when people counted you out and thought you were not going to accomplish the goal(s) that you set out to make. But God! Look at your now. With children, happily married, owning a business, buying a house, walking in peace, have a degree, and etc. You are resilient. You did not give up. You are still growing. Don't let statistics and society have the last word, you have the power to change. You have the power to continue to be resilient in this journey called life. You have the power to reflect on your journey. You my friend are growing. That is why you are understanding your resilience in the midst of growth.

Conclusion

When you are truly trying to change for the better, you will be tested. This is the only way you can recognize the growth you have received. After you have passed that test, then there will be something else that you need to address in order to grow. My husband and brother like to call this the process of elevation. You should always be willing to learn and grow from other people who may look different from you, have different beliefs and etc. Don't ever think of yourself as if you know it all, because at the end of the day you don't. Always remain humble. Understand that this journey called life you will have moments when you feel like you have it under control and then the next you are hit with a surprise. Friends, please have the mindset that you are always under construction. One way or another. Be willing to always humble yourself and be willing to have a heart that is willing to share the love, peace and joy that you have acquired throughout your life.

It is your responsibility to help others and guide them to the truth. Then once you have shared your journey with them, then they will decide if they are willing to make that decision for change. When I was in the process of writing this book trust and believe that I was tested in every aspect. It involved people that were closest to me. It required me to use the 5 c's to help other people change for the better. It required me and my husband to grow even closer in our relationship to one another, but most importantly with Christ.

Throughout the process of writing this book I remained opened to change in various situations and experiences. By me being open to change and applying the 5 c's I was able to try new things, read new books, discover the gifts, and talents. I was able to help others in the process. You have to remind yourself that change is a process. You have to understand that it is not a sprint and that you will always be fighting to keep that change consistent. When you are being tested, know that you will have to go back to the basic's, aka the foundation of your faith in Christ. Your foundation of praying, reading the word and praising God will help you while you are going through your storm and especially when you are trying to change for the better.

Dear Educators,

The beauty behind being in the field of education is that you have the love of learning. Even though we have the love of learning often times we as educators are quick to put our journey and experiences onto other students, but that is not the way we should think. We need to have compassion towards others. But, before you can have compassion towards others, you must have compassion with yourself.

With Kindness,

Angel

Resources and References

Center for Disease and Control Prevention. Preventing child abuse and neglect. (2019, February 26). Retrieved from https://www.cdc.gov/violenceprevention/childabuseandneglect/fastfact.html

The Glossary of Educational Reform. Growth Mindset. Great Schools Partnerships, 2013. Retrieved from https://www.edglossary.org/growth-mindset/

Jones Gunn, Robin and Goyer, Tricia. Praying for your future husband: Preparing your heart for his. Colorado Springs, Colorado. Multnomah Books. 2011.

Kacey, Martin. (2011, December 15). Trauma in the American Urban Classroom. Retrieved from https://edwp.educ.msu.edu/green-and-write/2015/trauma-in-the-american-urban-classroom/

Merriam-Webster.com Merriam-Webster, 2019. Web. 18, Aug 2019.

New International Version (NIV) Bible

About the Author

Dr. Angel Barber Jackson was born in Fort Riley, Kansas and raised in Jeffersonville, Indiana in a home of Christian principles. At the age of nineteen, she was called into ministry and pursued God's purpose for her life.

Dr. Jackson is a licensed and ordained minister who has preached at various churches since accepting her calling. She is also an Assistant Principal in one of the largest urban school districts in the United States where she has served as a passionate educator for change for over eleven years. As an educator, Dr. Jackson prides herself on building and sustaining positive relationships by supporting and advocating for students, teachers, staff, parents, and all stakeholders in doing what's best for students. According to Dr. Jackson:

> *"I believe in the power of change and the power of growth. In order to do so you must be willing to search within yourself and ask yourself, how can I become the leader that I would want to follow? If you are not willing to try something new, embrace something new, and understand the ability of new, then you are not ready for true change. I believe leadership is something that does not occur overnight, it is something that occurs daily, and should be evaluated in order to truly change any system. In order to do so, building positive relationships is essential to change!"*

Dr. Jackson lives in Southern Indiana with her husband, Brandon and their two children, Emerald and Braxton.

To contact Dr. Angel Barber Jackson, please send emails to: dr.angeljackson1985@gmail.com

www.ingramcontent.com/pod-product-compliance
Lightning Source LLC
Chambersburg PA
CBHW071415290426
44108CB00014B/1829